JONATHAN EVANS
ILLUSTRATIONS BY TODD HAMPSON

HARVEST HOUSE PUBLISHERS
EUGENE, OREGON

The quotation of Matthew 7:3-5 on page 216 is taken from the Holy Bible, New Living Translation, copyright © 1996, 2004, 2015 by Tyndale House Foundation. Used by permission of Tyndale House Publishers, Inc., Carol Stream, Illinois 60188. All rights reserved.

Cover design by Bryce Williamson

Interior design by Chad Dougherty

For bulk, special sales, or ministry purchases, please call 1-800-547-8979.
Email: Customerservice@hhpbooks.com

STORIES FROM THE STORYTELLER is a trademark of eLegacy Venture LLC.

This logo is a federally registered trademark of the Hawkins Children's LLC. Harvest House Publishers, Inc., is the exclusive licensee of this trademark.

Based on the *Stories from the Storyteller*™ video series, produced by Jonathan and Kanika Evans

The QR codes at the end of each chapter link to videos that are also available at these URLs:

https://tonyevans.org/storytellerintro	https://tonyevans.org/storyteller7
https://tonyevans.org/storyteller1	https://tonyevans.org/storyteller8
https://tonyevans.org/storyteller2	https://tonyevans.org/storyteller9
https://tonyevans.org/storyteller3	https://tonyevans.org/storyteller10
https://tonyevans.org/storyteller4	https://tonyevans.org/storyteller11
https://tonyevans.org/storyteller5	https://tonyevans.org/storyteller12
https://tonyevans.org/storyteller6	https://tonyevans.org/storytelleroutro

For questions regarding the QR codes, URLs, or videos, please visit tonyevans.org/contact.

Stories from the Storyteller™
Text copyright © 2023 by Jonathan Evans
Artwork © 2023 by Timbuktoons, LLC
Published by Harvest House Publishers
Eugene, Oregon 97408
www.harvesthousepublishers.com

ISBN 978-0-7369-8571-0 (hardcover)

Library of Congress Control Number: 2022938669

Printed in China

22 23 24 25 26 27 28 / RDS / 10 9 8 7 6 5 4 3 2 1

Contents

Introduction

HELLO, PARENTS, and thank you for using this book to help teach your kids some stories from the Storyteller. This book focuses on a few of the parables of Jesus—the greatest Storyteller of all time. We want your kids to be **begging for bedtime,** so we suggest reading a chapter to your children each night and then using the QR code provided so they can watch a bonus video on your device after each story is read from the book. We hope you enjoy *Stories from the Storyteller*™!

To scan the QR code at the end of each chapter:

Open the camera on your phone or tablet.

Aim it at the QR code.

Tap the banner that appears.

1

The Theme Park Prodigals

The entire Evans family, all seven of them, along with Tyson, their trusty dog, were stuffed into their van. Today was a big day. They were on their way to the wildest theme park in the state—perhaps even the country.

Kam squealed. "I've been waiting for decades for this day to come!"

"You're seven," Kelsey reminded him.

"It's just a theme park," J2 remarked.

Kylar stepped in. "It's not just any theme park, it's—"

The kids, along with their mom and dad, all shouted in unison, "The greeeaaat KING MOUNTAIN PARK OVER TEXAS!"

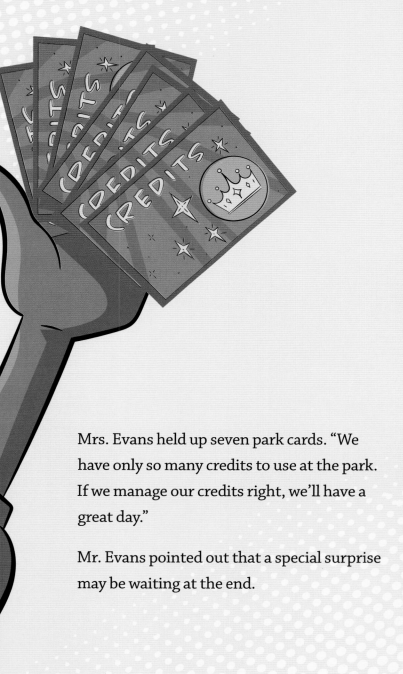

Mrs. Evans held up seven park cards. "We have only so many credits to use at the park. If we manage our credits right, we'll have a great day."

Mr. Evans pointed out that a special surprise may be waiting at the end.

The park was filled with all sorts of exciting things. Arcade games. Tasty food. And amazing roller coasters.

Kam and Kylar begged for their cards right away. "We wanna go to the arcade first," Kylar whined.

Mr. Evans reminded them to save their credits. "Once these are used up, that's it."

Kam and Kylar took off running for the games, barely listening.

Kylar and Kam sprinted from game to game. They both swiped their cards over and over, hoping to finally win the elusive stuffed panda and reach the next level.

Finally, the machines buzzed at the kids.
"What? No credits!" they both shouted.

Kylar and Kam found their mom and dad outside.

"I almost defeated the game! I need more credits," Kam pleaded.

Mr. Evans laughed. "You burned through all your credits in ten minutes?"

Mrs. Evans sighed. "I wish you would have let us manage your credits."

"Sorry, we got nothin' for ya," Mr. Evans stated as the family walked off.

Bored, Kam and Kylar sat on a park bench while their family enjoyed the fun rides.

It was finally the end of the day when J2 asked, "So what's the big surprise?"

"King Mountain Pizza Buffet!" Mr. Evans announced.

The hungry family went inside to eat the delicious, hot pizza—except for Kam and Kylar. They did not have the credits to get in.

Suddenly Mr. Evans appeared, holding two new cards of credits. "You guys hungry?"

Kylar and Kam ran and hugged their dad, feeling very grateful.

Kam and Kylar were excited to join their family for pizza.

J2 looked frustrated. "Why do they get to eat pizza?" he asked.

Kelsey added, "We saved our points! They shouldn't get to join in the surprise."

As the family entered their house that evening, Mr. Evans asked, "Hey kids, what time is it?"

Everyone shouted in unison, "STORYTIME!"

The kids quickly put on their superhero pajamas and piled onto their mom and dad's bed.

Mr. Evans began to tell a story. "Today reminded me of a parable Jesus told about a man who had two sons. The youngest son asked his father to give him half of everything he owned.

"The son quickly spent all of his inheritance on junk and couldn't even afford food. He was filled with regret and went home to apologize.

"The father saw his son coming and ran out to welcome and forgive him. He even threw him a huge party."

"The older brother didn't think it was fair and didn't join the party."

"God is always willing to wrap us in His arms, forgive us, and welcome us back home when we mess up," Mr. Evans explained.

"I'm sorry I got mad at you, Kam," J2 apologized.

"I'm sorry too, Kylar. At the time I thought it was unfair, but now I see that the Lord was using it to teach us both a big lesson," Kelsey added.

"I forgive you, Sis. Does this mean I can use some of that fancy perfume you got for Christmas?" Kylar asked.

"Don't push it, kid," responded Kelsey, smiling.

Mr. Evans looked around. "Hey, where's Bunny?" he asked.

The family found her under the bed with an empty box of pizza, looking a little sick.

"Easy-queasy," Bunny responded nauseously.

"Nooooooo!" they all screamed as they ran away.

2

Date-Night Return

CHORES

Mr. and Mrs. Evans were about to go on a date. They gathered everyone in the living room to say goodbye and to tell them some news.

"The house is a wreck, and our friends Delario and Lynzee Bowers are coming to visit tomorrow. So while we're gone, we need you to do some chores," Mr. Evans stated.

"I've gotta practice for tomorrow's e-sport tournament!" J2 protested.

Kelsey spoke up. "Paige and I were going to talk on the phone! I haven't talked to her in, like, 20 minutes!"

"Tyson, you're in charge. It's all about attitude, guys. Make it fun!" Mr. Evans reminded them.

Kam, Bunny, and Kylar were excited to get started on their chores, but J2 and Kelsey were not happy at all.

Kam pulled out a plate and made it roll up his arm, over his shoulder, and down to his hand. He flung the plate to Kylar.

Kylar caught it, did a fancy spin move, and then tossed it to Bunny, who caught the plate in mid-air. Amazingly, she placed the plate softly on the shelf.

Tyson walked through the schoolroom as Kelsey and J2 were cleaning. He approved and left the room.

Kelsey turned to J2 and said, "I know a way we can finish these chores faster so we can do what we really want. We don't necessarily have to clean; we can just create the *illusion* that we've cleaned."

J2 responded, "It's too risky, Kelsey. Besides, how would we fool Tyson?"

With loud music playing, Kyler mopped the wood floor. Bunny then spun on her back super fast, polishing the floor to a high shine.

Tyson was impressed by their quality of work and positive attitude.

"You have too much junk!" Kelsey snapped as she used all her weight to push J2's closet door shut.

"Me? You're the one with eight pairs of scissors," J2 replied. "Who needs eight pairs of scissors?"

As J2 dumped a basket of dirty clothes over Kelsey's head, a dirty sock landed on her face.

"Get it off! It smells like dead fish!" Kelsey screamed.

J2 noticed Tyson coming and shoved Kelsey into the closet.

Tyson looked at the seemingly clean room and then left.

"Sheew! That was close," exclaimed J2.

After stuffing everything into their closets, Kelsey jumped on the phone with her friend while J2 played Z-box. They had fooled everyone…or so they thought.

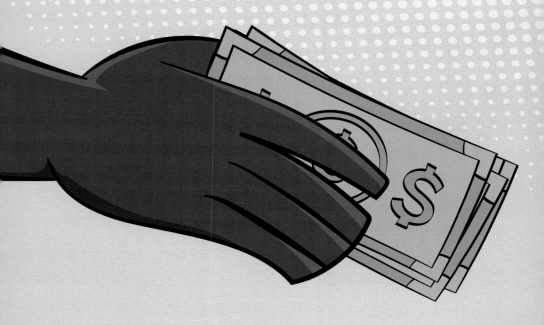

Later that evening, their parents looked around at the clean house. They were impressed by everyone's hard work.

"To show you our appreciation for cleaning the house, we're giving each of you five dollars," Mr. Evans announced.

The kids were super excited to hear this news!

J2 and Kelsey each stood at their bedroom doorways, smiling at their new five-dollar bills.

Suddenly, both of their closet doors burst open. An explosion of stinky clothes and craft supplies flew across their rooms and buried them both.

Mr. and Mrs. Evans were disappointed that J2 and Kelsey had lied about cleaning their rooms.

"Well, it's about that time," Mr. Evans said.

Everyone shouted in unison, "STORYTIME!"

The kids quickly put on their superhero pajamas and piled onto their mom and dad's bed.

Mr. Evans began to tell a story from the book of Matthew. "There was a man who was going on a long journey, and he entrusted his servants with his gold. He told them to use the money wisely.

"When the man returned and saw that the first two servants had doubled the money he had given them, he was pleased and responded, 'Well done good and faithful servants!' The man rewarded them both for their hard work."

"But when he found out the third servant had buried his money and had nothing to show for it, he was very upset and gave the money to one of the other servants."

"You see, guys, the Lord is expecting us to be faithful with what He has given us. We're not to be lazy and waste the gifts and talents He has given us to use."

Mr. Evans then asked J2 and Kelsey to give their five dollars to their brother and sisters. That day, they learned the importance of being faithful and trustworthy every single time.

3

Wilderness Wisdom

Mr. Evans walked into the living room and found the kids glued to their phones, playing games and texting friends.

"Hey kids, I think we need to get away from our devices. I have an idea! Let's go camping!"

"Nah, we're good, thanks," Kelsey replied as she quickly typed away on her phone.

"I think camping is a great idea!" Mrs. Evans expressed.

"Wait, is camping outside?" J2 asked.

"You seriously just asked that? Yes, of course it's outside—
in God's beautiful creation! And we're all going!" Mr. Evans
was excited.

The kids whined and pouted about the idea of camping until Mrs. Evans said, "You can bring two friends." Suddenly, camping sounded like an amazing idea to the kids.

The next day, the kids brought their friends Joel Chein and Ellie to the backyard to meet with Mr. Evans, who had four tents in different colors.

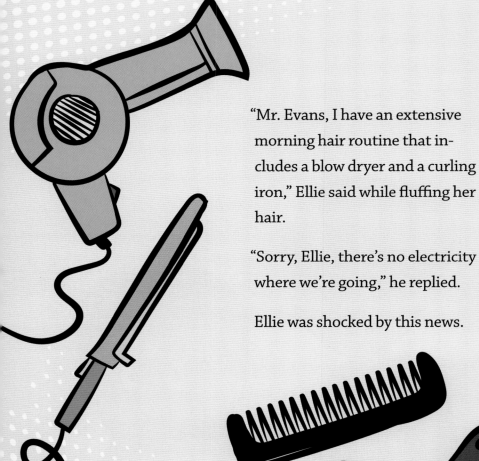

"Mr. Evans, I have an extensive morning hair routine that includes a blow dryer and a curling iron," Ellie said while fluffing her hair.

"Sorry, Ellie, there's no electricity where we're going," he replied.

Ellie was shocked by this news.

"Okay, guys, a properly pitched tent can make or break a camping trip. So we're going to go over five fundamentals of setting up a tent," Mr. Evans explained.

"It's a tent, Dad. Just tie it to a tree and go chase skunks," Kam said.

Mr. Evans responded, "It's not that easy, and no one is chasing skunks, okay?"

"Fundamental number one: Always practice pitching the tent before getting to the campsite," Mr. Evans explained.

"The second fundamental is to choose a good flat spot to set up your tent."

"Next, tie the tent ropes to a good strong tree," Mr. Evans said while tying a firm knot.

"The fourth fundamental is to always remember to stake the tent to the ground."

"And finally, make sure you
don't put your tent in a place
where something can fall on
it in the middle of the night."

"You mean like a meteor?"
Kam asked.

"Yeah! Or a spaceship?" Joel added.

"No, like a tree limb," Mr. Evans replied.

"Oh, right," Kam smiled.

Everyone was excited when they arrived at the campsite. In fact, they were so excited that Kam and Joel quickly tied their tent to a tree and then ran off to go fishing. The girls, excited about chasing bunny rabbits, quickly set up their tent over bumpy roots in the ground.

That night, a big storm moved over the campsite. Because Kam and Joel's tent wasn't staked to the ground, the wind picked it up. It flapped like a wet flag.

The girls had forgotten fundamental number two and were unable to sleep because of the bumpy ground. They crawled out of their tent just as a limb crashed on it. Apparently, they had forgotten rule number five as well.

J2 and Tyson had followed all five fundamentals and were warm and cozy in their tent, playing card games and eating snacks.

It was a very long and wet night for those who didn't follow the five fundamentals.

The next day, the Evans family walked into their house ready
for long, hot showers.

"Well, at least there's one good thing to look forward to,"
stated J2, and everyone shouted in unison, "STORYTIME!"

The kids quickly put on their superhero pajamas and piled
onto their mom and dad's bed.

Mr. Evans began to tell a story from the book of Matthew. "Jesus said, 'Anyone who puts My words into practice is like a wise man who built his house on rock. But anyone who doesn't put them into practice is like a foolish man who built his house on sand. When the rains came down, the house fell with a big crash.'

"The rock is God's Word, and it can't be moved or broken like sand. Jesus wants us to build our lives on His Word so we can weather life's storms."

"I'm sorry we totally ignored your fundamentals, Dad," Kylar responded.

"We sure learned a lot!" Kam replied.

"Anyone hear something squeaky?" asked Bunny.

Suddenly, Kam's new pet skunk popped out, smiled, and gave a cute little squeak. Then he reared his fluffy tail, ready to spray them.

"No, Mr. Cologne! You promised!" Kam yelled.

"Everybody ruuuuuuun!" Mr. Evans shouted.

4

The Sugar Monster

J2, Kylar, Kelsey, Kam, and Bunny were seated at the kitchen table talking over each other in excitement when their dad walked in.

"What's all the excitement about?" Mr. Evans asked.

"It's Halloween, Dad!" Kelsey responded.

Kam stood up and declared, "The best holiday ever!"

"Besides Easter and Christmas, obviously," Kylar added.

"Trading candy is the best part!" J2 cried.

"Last year Mrs. Stevenson gave out string. What are we supposed to do with that?" Kam asked.

"That was dental floss," Kelsey answered.

"I wonder if Mr. Nichols will give out those big candy bars again," Kylar asked.

"Now, *those* were fun sized!" J2 exclaimed.

"Okay, people, let's focus!" Kelsey interrupted.

Everyone got quiet. Suddenly, out of nowhere, Kelsey whipped out a poster and unrolled it across the kitchen table. "We have a lot of houses to hit in a short amount of time. I've mapped out the fastest route based on step count, shortcuts, and stride. We hit them hard, and we hit them fast!"

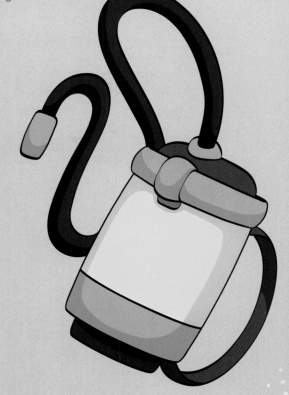

"Well, you guys better get started on your costumes," Mrs. Evans reminded.

While everyone was distracted and making their costumes, Kelsey quietly snuck up to the hallway closet, grabbed the vacuum, and pulled it into her bathroom.

"Tonight is going to be epic!" she said, grinning from ear to ear.

The neighborhood was abuzz with pirates, fairies, and silly monsters running from house to house trick-or-treating. The Evans kids were all dressed up and ready to go.

"Okay, so here's the plan: I'll run up ahead and make sure the candy is good, and then I'll let you know," Kelsey said. Before anyone could reply, Kelsey took off like a rocket, leaving her brothers and sisters behind.

Kelsey approached a house that had a bowl of candy sitting on the stoop with a sign that read, "Take one please."

She reached her hand down into the bowl. The vacuum that she had hidden under her cape began to suck all the candy out of the bowl. "Ha ha, it works!" Kelsey shouted.

Kelsey ran to the next house. Kam, Kylar, J2, and Bunny walked up to find only three pieces of candy left.

After finding only a small amount of candy at each house, Kylar spoke up. "Why are people being so stingy with the candy this year?"

"Yeah, don't they know *all* my teeth are sweet tooths?" Kam exclaimed.

Kelsey continued running from house to house, sucking up nearly all the candy and leaving very little for the others.

The kids were very gloomy when they got home. Kelsey sneaked up to the attic and found an old box to hide all her candy in.

"Tonight I shall dine on any candy I wish," Kelsey declared.

Later, Mr. Evans needed help clearing out some boxes from the attic. He handed everyone a box to carry to the trash. Kelsey realized the box she was holding was the very box where she had hidden all her candy.

As they approached the trash can at the street, Mr. Evans told Kelsey, "I think I want to keep that box. Just dump the contents into the trash."

Kelsey knew she was in trouble. She slowly opened the box and dumped all her candy into the trash can. As her brothers and sisters watched the enormous amount of candy fall out, they became furious.

"Why did you do that, Kelsey?" Kam asked.

"The best part of Halloween is trading candy," J2 cried.

"I didn't want to trade. I just wanted it all to myself," Kelsey explained.

When Kelsey saw the glum look on her brothers' and sisters' faces, she felt horrible about what she had done.

STORYTIME!

"It's getting late. I think it's time," Mrs. Evans announced.

"STORYTIME!" the kids yelled.

All the kids got into their superhero pajamas and piled onto their parents' bed.

Mr. Evans began to tell a story from the Bible. "Jesus told a story about a rich man who had too much grain. Instead of giving the extra to those in need, he decided to keep it all to himself. Jesus said the man was a fool for storing everything for himself, rather than being rich toward God."

"He was only thinking of himself," J2 observed.

Kelsey spoke up, "Just like I was only thinking about what I wanted and how I could have all the candy to myself. Believe me, it was not worth it."

"Jesus tells us that life is not about having a whole lot of stuff. It's more important to share with others," Mr. Evans added.

Everyone forgave Kelsey that night, and she learned that honesty and loving others are so much better than being selfish.

5

Cook-Off Competition Catastrophe

Mrs. Evans walked into the schoolroom to see all the kids looking very bored. "Looks like you guys could use a little break," she observed.

"We sure could! Can I go to the mall?" Kelsey asked.

"I want to go over to Sarah's house," Kylar begged.

"I have good news! Poppy and Nonny are coming for din-ner," Mrs. Evans announced. Everyone was very excited about seeing their grandparents.

"I thought we'd have a little cooking competition between you all. Meet me in the kitchen," she directed.

All the kids stood in the kitchen wearing aprons, looking through their mother's recipe book.

"Find a recipe in this cookbook that you think Poppy and Nonny would like. And remember, it's very important that you follow these recipes exactly. Ready, set, COOK!"

The kids clamored over each other to get to the refrigerator and pantry. They quickly gathered all the ingredients they needed to make their dishes.

As J2 was stirring sugar into his brownie mix, he looked up to find his cousin Joshua filming him with his camera.

"Joshua, why are you filming me?" J2 asked.

"Your mom asked me to come over and film the show," Joshua replied.

Joshua filmed Kelsey mixing her ingredients. "Poppy and Nonny are going to love my soft and delicious chocolate chip cookies," Kelsey said.

She dipped her finger in the batter to taste it. Her face turned a funny shade of green.

Joshua filmed Kam dropping one tomato into the saucepot. "Spaghetti sauce is done," he said proudly.

Bunny was focused as she whisked a bowl of flour. She added a little salt, tasted it, and then winked at the camera.

FIVE MINUTES!

"Five minutes!" Mrs. Evans announced.

"What? Five minutes?" everyone shouted.

Poppy and Nonny arrived and were seated at the dining room table along with Mr. and Mrs. Evans. Kam and Kylar were up first.

"Hey, Poppy and Nonny. We have your favorite—chicken parmesan!" Kylar announced.

Poppy grinned. "Oh boy, I do love chicken parmesan!"

"You kids have been busy in the kitchen," Nonny said.

Kam and Kylar placed a frozen chicken patty on each person's plate, along with a helping of uncooked spaghetti noodles on top. They had forgotten to read the part of the recipe about cooking the chicken and noodles.

J2 was next. As he walked in, everyone was surprised that he was holding an empty mixing bowl.

"I made you all brownies for dessert. But I kind of ate all the batter," he said.

"I'm sure they were delicious," Nonny replied graciously.

Kelsey announced, "Lucky for you, I made soft and delicious chocolate chip cookies."

When her grandparents took a bite, it sounded like they were eating hard crackers, not soft, warm cookies. Kelsey also had not read the recipe fully.

Bunny walked in with an enormous loaf of bread stuffed with hot and delicious pork tenderloin.

"Bread with meat inside? That's the most beautiful thing I've ever seen," Poppy exclaimed.

Everyone enjoyed Bunny's dish because she had followed the recipe exactly.

"Well, I think we can declare Bunny the winner because she made something we could actually chew," Mrs. Evans announced.

"It's getting late. Poppy, would you like to do storytime tonight?" Mr. Evans asked.

"I would love to," Poppy replied.

"STORYTIME!" everyone yelled.

STORYTIME!

"You know, your creations tonight reminded me of a parable Jesus told about a farmer who went out to sow his seed. As he was scattering the seed, some fell along the path where it was trampled on, and the birds ate it up. Other seed fell among weeds, which eventually choked the good plants. Other seed fell on good soil, where they grew a hundred times more than what was sown."

"You see, the Bible is like a recipe for good and healthy living. When we follow it, we live productive and joyful lives. When we don't follow God's Word, we tend to live hard and unfulfilling lives."

"Kinda like my cookies," Kelsey responded.

"Or like our frozen chicken parmesan," Kam stated.

Poppy chuckled and said, "Well, yes. You guys didn't follow the recipe, and the results were not great. But Jesus tells us that if we read His Word, it's like eating really warm and delicious food…we will be full and comforted."

6
The Sly Seed Sower

One day, as the Evans kids were doing their schoolwork, Mrs. Evans announced, "Today we are going to learn about seeds and how they grow."

The kids were excited and crowded around their mom to get a closer look at the small seeds in her palm.

"So tiny," Bunny said.

"I thought seeds were bigger," Kam added.

"Seeds come in all shapes and sizes. God designed each seed to grow a certain plant or tree, and you guys are going to watch it happen," Mrs. Evans explained.

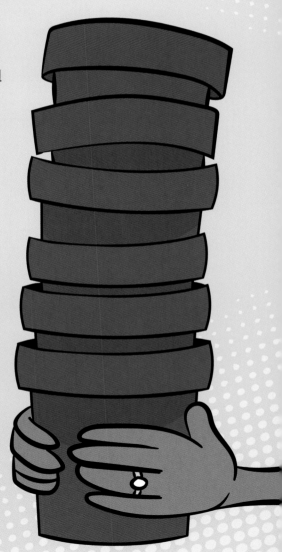

They were all very excited to see how seeds worked.

Mrs. Evans continued, "I'm going to give each of you a vegetable or a fruit seed, and you're going to plant it in your own pot."

"I hope I get one that grows chocolate," Kylar announced.

"Chocolate doesn't grow on trees," J2 said.

Kelsey, J2, and Kam began to laugh at her.

Kylar felt embarrassed, but Mrs. Evans said, "Well, actually it does."

Everyone stopped laughing.

"The cocoa tree produces large seeds that farmers pick and dry. The dried seeds are then turned into chocolate," Mrs. Evans explained.

Kylar certainly did not appreciate being laughed at.

"Is there anything that will keep the seeds from growing?" Kam inquired.

"Yes, weeds. Weeds will steal a plant's sunlight and nutri-ents and eventually kill it," Mrs. Evans explained.

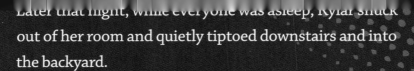

Later that night, while everyone was asleep, Kylar snuck out of her room and quietly tiptoed downstairs and into the backyard.

She began to walk around the yard with a flash-light. "There's got to be one around here somewhere," she said.

Suddenly Kylar spotted a big, ugly weed poking out of the grass. Kylar reached down and pulled it from the ground. "Perfect!" she said.

Kylar then walked over to the pots where her brothers and sisters had planted their seeds and began to shake the weed. Tiny little weed seeds rained down over the soil.

"That'll teach them to laugh at me," Kylar said.

A week went by, and the tiny seeds the children had planted began to sprout. Everyone was excited to see whether they were growing a vegetable or a fruit.

One morning, they all decided to walk outside and check on their plants. They were shocked when they found huge, mean-looking weeds pouring out of their pots.

"That's a weird-looking fruit!" Kam exclaimed.

"That's no fruit. That's a weed!" J2 shouted.

"I don't understand. We put them up on tables so weeds couldn't reach them," Mrs. Evans said.

Kylar walked over to her pot to see a flower poking up through the soil.

"Hey! How come Kylar doesn't have any weeds?" Kelsey asked.

Kylar held her pot and shrugged her shoulders, smiling innocently.

Bunny looked up at the ugly weed and began to cry. When Kylar saw Bunny crying and her brothers and sisters looking sad, she began to feel guilty about what she had done.

"It was me," Kylar confessed.

"Why did you do that?" Mrs. Evans asked.

"I was upset that everyone laughed at
me about the chocolate tree.
I wanted to get back at them,"
Kylar explained.

Mrs. Evans suggested, "Well, let's all go inside and get ready for—"

"Bedtime?" Kam interrupted.

Kelsey added, "And bedtime means…"

"STORYTIME!" everyone shouted in unison.

Mr. Evans began to tell a story from the Bible.

"Jesus told a parable that seems like a good fit for today.
He said the kingdom of heaven is like a man who sowed
good seed in his field. But while everyone was sleeping, his
enemy came and sowed weeds among the wheat."

"The farmer instructed his servants to let both grow together until the harvest. Then he told them to collect the weeds and tie them in bundles to be burned. Next, they were to gather the wheat and bring it into the barn."

"What does that parable mean?" asked Kam.

"There's going to be a time when the Lord is going to separate the good plants—His children—from the weeds—those who hate Him. God is full of grace, forgiveness, and patience, but He is a holy God who must eventually punish evil. It's a great reminder that God has a plan."

"I'm so sorry for letting my anger get the best of me and for ruining your plants. Will you guys forgive me?" Kylar asked.

"Of course we do," J2 replied.

Everyone forgave Kylar and gave her a big hug.

7

The Creek Creature

113

The family was in the living room watching J2 put on a magic show. Kam and Kylar were mesmerized as he dramatically cut open an orange to reveal a rolled-up playing card inside.

J2 showed Mr. Evans the card and asked, "Is this the card you saw?"

Mr. Evans smiled and responded, "Nope."

"What? It's not the two of spades?" J2 asked.

"Sorry, it was the king of hearts," Mr. Evans replied.

"Keep practicing, sweetheart. The disappearing milk trick was cool. I'm sure most of it will come out of the carpet," Mrs. Evans said.

"You know, it's a beautiful day. We should all go outside," Mr. Evans said.

"We found a creek behind our house!" Kam exclaimed.

"Well, let's go explore it!" Mr. Evans responded.

"I'm not going," J2 announced.

"Why not?" Kam asked.

J2 replied, "The creek creature."

"Oh, stop. There's no creek creature. Let's go on a family adventure," Mrs. Evans said.

The family walked into the thick forest behind their house. They approached a steep and slick embankment and carefully made their way down.

At the bottom of the hill, they found a tiny creek. The family followed the creek deeper into the forest.

After walking along the creek for a while, J2 announced, "I'm feeling tired, so I'm going to head back home. You guys have fun!"

The rest of the family continued and enjoyed jumping from rock to rock and walking across fallen trees along the creek.

After having fun in the creek, they returned to the steep embankment. Tyson began to growl at something.

Suddenly, a mound of leaves began to rise up from the ground.

"CREEK CREATURE!" Kam shouted.

Everyone's eyes got huge as the creek creature began to moan...but then started laughing.

"Why is it laughing?" Kelsey asked.

Kelsey walked over to the creek creature and pulled off a sheet that leaves were glued to, revealing J2 underneath, laughing hysterically.

"J2!" everyone shouted.

"You should have seen your faces!" J2 exclaimed.

Suddenly, Tyson began growling again.

"Tyson, it's just J2," Kelsey said.

"Look!" Kam yelled.

A large raccoon stood
directly behind J2 and snarled.

"CREEK CREATURE!" J2 screamed.

Everyone tried to run up the steep embankment, but the grass was wet and their feet kept slipping.

"We need help, Dad!" Kelsey screamed out.

Mr. and Mrs. Evans sprang into action, quickly pulling each kid up the hill.

Finally, everyone was up, safe from the grumpy raccoon.

Later that evening, when the family had finished dinner, J2 and Kylar began to clear the table and wash the dishes. Bunny stood on a chair and massaged Mrs. Evans's shoulders.

"They're just being nice because you saved them on the hill," Kam exclaimed.

"Oh really? And you didn't need my help?" responded Mr. Evans.

"I was about to roundhouse kick that raccoon. We were fine," Kelsey stated.

"You know, this would be a good topic to discuss at bedtime," Mrs. Evans said.

Mr. Evans added, "And bedtime means…"

"STORYTIME!" everyone screamed in unison.

"We sure had an adventure today, kids. Jesus told this story to a Pharisee named Simon: 'Two people owed money to a man. One owed him 500 denarii, and the other owed 50, but neither of them had the money to pay him back, so he forgave the debts of both. Now which of them will love him more?' Simon answered, 'I suppose the one who had the bigger debt forgiven.' 'You have judged correctly,' Jesus replied."

"Kelsey and Kam, your brothers and sisters were grateful to your mother and me for helping them up the hill today, and they showed their gratitude by helping and serving us. Were you guys thankful?"

"No, sir," Kelsey responded. "I didn't realize how prideful I was acting. Even though I needed help too, I acted like I was better than them. I'm sorry, Mom and Dad."

"I'm sorry too!" Kam said.

"We forgive you guys!" Mr. Evans said.

"You know, Jesus will always save us when we call out to Him. We give Him our best to show our gratitude for Him dying for our sins."

8

Reckless Responsibility

The Evans kids walked into their living room and took a seat on the couch. Mr. Evans had just called a family meeting.

"Since you guys are getting older and becoming more mature, we feel it's time to give you more responsibilities," Mr. Evans announced.

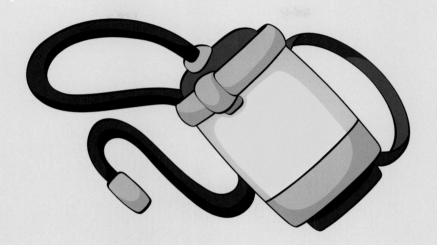

"J2, you and Kelsey are going to cut the bushes and blow off the driveway," Mr. Evans said.

"Kam, Kylar, and Bunny, you guys are going to get some big-kid responsibilities, like vacuuming, dusting, and making your bed," Mrs. Evans added. "Your dad and I are headed to the grocery store and will be back soon."

The kids got right to their new responsibilities. Kam vacuumed, Kylar put fresh sheets on the beds, and Bunny dusted the furniture.

Outside, J2 was cutting the bushes while Kelsey blew the leaves off the driveway. J2 noticed that she was unable to get the leaves out from under the car.

"We are close to being able to drive, ya know," J2 said.

Kelsey smiled. She knew what J2 was thinking.

Back inside, Kam noticed J2's really cool Z-box console. "Mom and Dad did say I was more mature now. Hey, Kylar, wanna play?"

The pair began to play Z-box while eating some chocolate candy they found in J2's dresser.

J2 and Kelsey drove slowly to the end of the driveway and stopped.

"Surely Mom and Dad will be fine with us parking on the street," J2 said.

"Totally. Like they said, we're mature now," Kelsey reminded him.

While Kam and Kylar played J2's Z-box, Bunny was dusting in Kelsey's room. Meanwhile, she became a little too curious with some of Kelsey's craft projects.

J2 and Kelsey were driving down the street when a squirrel suddenly jumped out in front of the car. J2 swerved and plowed directly into the neighbor's mailbox.

Right then, Mr. and Mrs. Evans pulled up. They were shocked to find J2, Kelsey, and their car in the neighbor's yard.

As Kam and Kylar finished their game, they suddenly noticed chocolate all over the Z-box.

Kam had an idea. He picked up the console, ran to the bathroom, and washed off the chocolate into the sink.

"You guys are going to have to sell your Z-box and craft cutter to pay for the car repair and a new mailbox." Mr. Evans explained to J2 and Kelsey.

The pair fell to their knees and begged not to have to sell their favorite things. Mr. Evans saw their genuine remorse and had grace on them.

"Maybe Uncle Anthony can fix the bumper, and I'll pay for the mailbox," Mr. Evans said.

J2 and Kelsey thanked their dad repeatedly. They were grateful they didn't have to sell their favorite things.

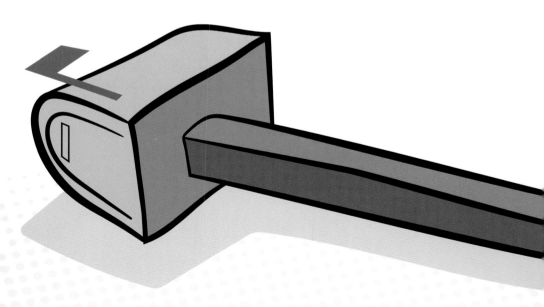

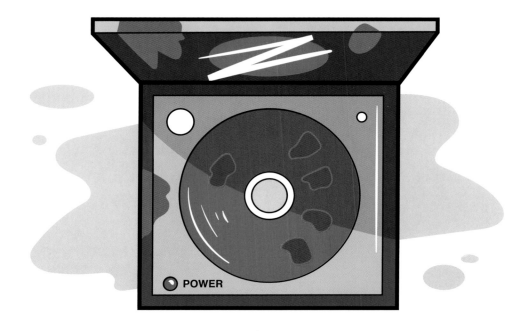

Later, when J2 got back to his room, he noticed his Z-box was wet and completely ruined. He became angry at Kam and Kylar.

When Kelsey walked into her room and found her craft projects destroyed, she became angry at Bunny as well.

Mr. Evans confronted them, "J2 and Kelsey, how could you not forgive your brother and sister, after I just forgave you of an even bigger offense?" Mr. Evans asked.

The pair didn't have an answer.

"Now you're going to have to pay for the car repairs and the mailbox, and you're grounded for two weeks," Mr. Evans explained.

Later that evening as they gathered on their parents' bed for storytime, Mr. Evans began to read a parable from the Bible.

"There was a man who owed the king a lot of gold. The man fell on his knees before the king and begged for mercy. The king took pity on him and let him go free."

"But when that man left, he confronted a friend who owed him a smaller amount of money. But the friend couldn't pay, so the man threw his friend into prison until he could pay the debt.

"When the king heard this, he was furious and said to the man, 'I canceled all of your debt. Shouldn't you have had mercy on your friend just as I had mercy on you?'"

"Kids, Jesus died for our sin and canceled our debt. We should likewise show grace to others when they offend us," Mr. Evans explained.

J2 and Kelsey apologized to their brother and sisters for becoming angry. That day they learned firsthand a big lesson about demonstrating grace to others.

9

Pick to Play

J2, Kam, Kelsey, Kylar, and Bunny were staring out the window, watching their mom and dad do sit-ups, push-ups, and yoga, all while holding a Frisbee.

"What are Mom and Dad doing?" Kam asked.

"They're getting ready to play chicken Frisbee. It's like football but with a Frisbee," Kelsey explained.

"Every year, Uncle Anthony, Aunt Chrystal, and Aunt Priscilla compete against Mom and Dad in chicken Frisbee," J2 continued.

"Is there a chicken?" Bunny asked.

"No. You'll have to watch and see," said Kelsey.

Later that day, the Evans family arrived at the park where they met their grandparents, Poppy and Nonny.

"Hey kids, it's so good to see you!" Poppy said.

"Oh, how I love hugs from these sweet grandkids of mine!" Nonny exclaimed.

Uncle Anthony, Aunt Chrystal, and Aunt Priscilla were already in the long, grassy field warming up for the big game. Mr. and Mrs. Evans took their place on the opposite side of the field.

Uncle Anthony slipped a sweatband over his forehead.

"I thought those went out of style in the eighties," Mr. Evans joked.

"You know I have extra sweat glands!" Uncle Anthony responded.

Poppy stood up and revealed the golden trophy of a chicken holding a Frisbee on top. "Okay, the winner gets to take home the chicken Frisbee trophy," Poppy announced.

Nonny blew a whistle, and the game began.

Mr. Evans threw the Frisbee to Mrs. Evans. As she ran with it, Aunt Priscilla quickly tagged her.

The game was really heating up as Mr. Evans ran past everyone and made it across the goal line. Mr. and Mrs. Evans began to do the chicken victory dance.

"And that's why they call it chicken Frisbee," Kelsey explained.

Later in the game, Mr. Evans looked over to see Aunt Priscilla coming at him.

"I'm coming for you!" Aunt Priscilla shouted.

Mr. Evans quickly threw the Frisbee to Mrs. Evans, but she had to jump to catch it. When Mrs. Evans landed, she twisted her ankle and had to sit down on the sideline. The kids were called in to take her place.

J2, Kelsey, Kylar, and Kam all had a chance to play. They even scored a few points. They especially enjoyed doing the chicken victory dance.

The score was tied, and it was Bunny and Tyson's turn to play.

Tyson had the Frisbee and was running frantically. He was looking for Bunny, but she was twirling, giggling, and not paying attention. Tyson threw it toward Bunny just as Aunt Priscilla tackled him.

Everyone gasped when the Frisbee flew through the air and landed in Bunny's hair! She giggled, tripped on her shoelace, and fell across the goal line. They won the game!

Back home, Aunt Priscilla brought out a pan of her famous cinnamon rolls and began passing them out to everyone. This special treat was reserved for those who had played chicken Frisbee.

"How come Bunny and Tyson get a cinnamon roll?" J2 griped. "They were only in the game for one play. We scored more points and played a lot longer."

"Maybe Poppy can discuss this at storytime," suggested Mr. Evans.

"STORYTIME!" everyone shouted in unison.

All the kids piled onto the couch around Poppy and Nonny.

Poppy began, "Jesus told a parable about a man who owned a vineyard. He went out and hired some men in the morning to work in his fields. Then, around noon he hired some more workers. He went out two more times in the afternoon and hired workers. At the end of the day, he paid each worker the exact same wage."

"Then Jesus said something very important: 'So the last will be first, and the first will be last.'

"Regardless of how long you've been a Christian, the reward of eternal life with Jesus is the same for us all," Poppy said.

"Just like the cinnamon rolls," observed Kam.

"That's right. Some of you played for a long time and some of you played for a short time, but everyone got the same reward because that's what your mom and dad wanted to do," Poppy concluded.

"I know that Tyson and Bunny were thankful they did," responded Kelsey.

Everyone looked at Bunny, who was running around in circles with an empty tray in her hand.

"Oh no—how many cinnamon rolls has she eaten?" Mrs. Evans questioned.

Bunny suddenly looked very nauseous.

Mr. Evans yelled, "Ruuuuun!"

10

The Good Samaritan

One lazy afternoon, the kids were all in their rooms playing with toys, video games, and crafts. Mr. Evans was in the living room cleaning when suddenly a cat climbed up his leg and parked on top of his head.

Mr. Evans began to do the "What's on my head?" dance.

"It's just Mr. Belvedere, the neighbor's cat," said Mrs. Evans calmly.

Suddenly, Tyson came flying into the living room and chased Mr. Belvedere through the house and out into the backyard. The family watched as the pair ran, barked, and hissed at each other.

"I don't think they like each other," Kam observed.

"One time I found Tyson on my phone texting animal control to come get a ferocious baby lion in the yard," Kelsey explained.

"Tyson can text?" asked Mr. Evans.

"All the time," Kelsey shared.

Mrs. Evans said, "I think I have an idea of how we can help Tyson."

The family walked to the local dog park, where there were big dogs, little dogs who thought they were big dogs, and a group of poodles who didn't like the dirt on the ground.

"I think Tyson just needs to learn how to play well with others," Mrs. Evans said.

Tyson walked up to three very large dogs named Magnus, Hank, and PeeWee. Magnus was the leader of the group.

"Hey guys, I'm Tyson," he said.

"I've never seen you here before," Magnus replied.

"It's my first time. You guys wanna play?" Tyson asked.

"Sure kid, you can play with us," Magnus said, grinning mischievously.

Tyson chased Magnus, PeeWee, and Hank all over the park. Then Magnus and his gang ran through a tunnel.

As Tyson was running full speed through the tunnel, Magnus and his gang dropped a wooden board in front of the opening.

Tyson couldn't stop in time and busted through the board. He laid on the ground, dizzy, as the gang laughed at him. A group of poodles walked by and saw the lump on Tyson's head, but they didn't stop to help.

While chasing a ball, PeeWee knocked Tyson into a fence next to the chihuahuas. He was stuck and needed help, but the chihuahuas just walked away.

Then they all noticed a woman handing out doggy treats. While Tyson waited his turn for a treat, Magnus and the gang snuck up and stole the rest of the treats without her noticing.

"Wow, I'm out of treats already. Sorry, guys," said the woman.

Tyson noticed that Magnus had a big pile of treats.

"Can I have one?" Tyson asked.

Tyson reached out to take a treat when Magnus, Hank, and PeeWee jumped up and growled at him. He was frozen with fear.

Suddenly, out of nowhere, Mr. Belvedere jumped in front of Tyson and hissed at the mean gang, showing his sharp teeth.

Magnus screamed, PeeWee jumped into Hank's arms, and all three ran off, scared. Mr. Belvedere relaxed and licked his paw.

"Thank you!" Tyson said gratefully.

Mr. Belvedere tossed a doggy treat to Tyson and walked off.

Later that night, the kids and Tyson were all piled on their parents' bed, ready for storytime.

"I think Tyson will appreciate this parable. It's about the good Samaritan," Mr. Evans shared.

"Jesus told a story about a man who was attacked by robbers. They took everything he had, beat him up, and left him in the street badly hurt. Several people walked past the man, but no one stopped to help him."

LUKE 10:25-37

"Then a Samaritan saw the hurt man and felt bad for him. He bandaged his wounds and took him to an inn, where he was taken care of until he was healed.

"Jesus asks us to love our neighbor just like we want to be loved," Mr. Evans concluded.

"So our neighbor is anyone who needs help?" Kelsey asked.

"That's right, Kelsey," Mr. Evans responded.

"How do I love my online friends? I don't see them," asked J2.

"Well, if you notice that a friend seems down, you could offer some encouragement and then check up on them later to make sure they are doing okay," Mr. Evans suggested.

"Great idea!" J2 exclaimed.

Suddenly, a cat screeched loudly outside. Tyson's ears popped up. He smiled and then took off outside.

The family watched as Tyson and Mr. Belvedere happily chased each other around the yard.

Later that evening, Mr. Evans received a selfie from Tyson and Mr. Belvedere with big smiles.

11

Birthday Party Prestige

The Evans family was sitting at the kitchen table eating breakfast when Kelsey suddenly squealed loudly.

"What is it, Kelsey?" Kam asked

"I just got invited to Paige's birthday party! Actually, it looks like you're all invited," Kelsey announced.

"I'm not interested in going to a girl's birthday party," responded J2.

"It's at Adventure Land," shared Kelsey.

The entire family jumped up and started doing a happy dance—even Mr. Evans.

"I've never seen a grown man so excited about a teenage girl's birthday party," Mrs. Evans said.

Mr. Evans stopped dancing and tried to play it cool.

"It could be fun…you know, for the kids," Mr. Evans explained.

The family walked into Adventure Land. The place was abuzz with kids having a great time playing arcade games.

They spotted Paige and all said, "Happy birthday, Paige!"

"Thank you guys for coming. Let's go ride go-karts!" Paige
suggested.

"Let's get this party started!" yelled Mr. Evans.

Everyone stopped and looked at Mr. Evans. He smiled, a
bit embarrassed.

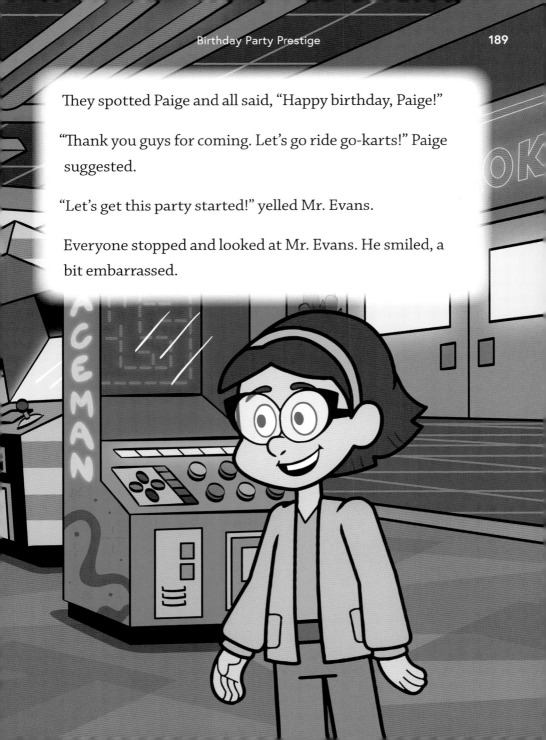

As everyone was choosing a go-kart, J2 ran in front of Paige to get the first one.

Kam saw what J2 had done. "Hey, Paige, take this one," Kam said as he got out of his go-kart, which was closer to the front.

J2's plan was to be the first to cross the finish line. But his go-kart was the slowest on the track.

After racing go-karts, Paige and the birthday crowd walked into a room with a small stage and microphone. Kelsey overheard Paige tell a friend, "You're not going to believe who my mom got to sing 'Happy Birthday.'"

"It must be me! I guess her mom forgot to ask," Kelsey said to herself.

Kelsey rushed the stage and took the microphone from Paige's mom.

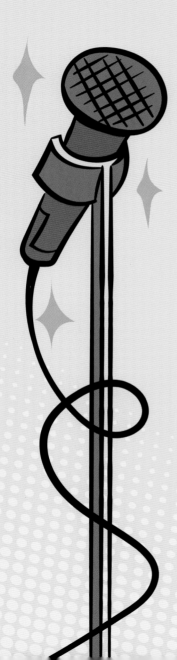

Just as Kelsey was about to sing, Mrs. Conner leaned into Kelsey's ear and whispered, "Kelsey, we hired Bella, a professional singer, to sing."

Kelsey tried to hide her embarrassment. "Ha ha...just a little joke for your birthday, Paige," she stammered.

After singing, everyone got in line for birthday cake. When Bunny saw the huge cake, she walked past everyone, including Paige, and tried to stick her finger in the icing. Mrs. Evans scooped her up and walked her to the end of the long line. Bunny was not happy when she received the last piece, which was paper thin.

Paige approached Kam. "I noticed you took the last go-kart so I could be closer to the front. And you gave me the corner piece of the birthday cake—my favorite."

"It's your birthday. You should feel special," Kam responded.

"I could use some assistance unwrapping gifts. Want to help me out?" asked Paige.

"Yeah!" Kam responded.

Kam proudly stood at the table and cut ribbon so Paige could easily open the presents.

Later that evening, everyone sat in the living room, tired from the full day of fun.

"What a great party!" Kam exclaimed.

"I made a fool of myself," Kelsey responded.

"Yeah, me too," J2 echoed.

Mrs. Evans reminded, "Well, it's getting late. I think it's…"

"STORYTIME!" everyone shouted in unison.

The kids gathered on the couch, ready for storytime.

Mr. Evans said, "Today I was reminded of a parable Jesus told in the book of Luke. He said, when someone invites you to a wedding feast, do not take the place of honor, because someone more important may arrive. Then the host will ask you to move to the least important seat, and you'll be embarrassed."

LUKE 14

"Instead, take the least important seat so the host will invite you to a better seat. Then you will be honored in the presence of all the other guests. For all those who exalt themselves will be humbled, and those who humble themselves will be exalted," Mr. Evans concluded.

"I was the opposite of humble today, thinking I was the special singer," remarked Kelsey.

"And it was selfish of me to take the first go-kart instead of giving it to Paige," J2 responded.

"Jesus is reminding us in this parable that when we humble ourselves and think of others first, it actually works in our favor, and we become the honored ones," Mr. Evans said.

"Kam put Paige first today," Kelsey observed.

"He got rewarded for it too. Good job, little bro!" encouraged J2.

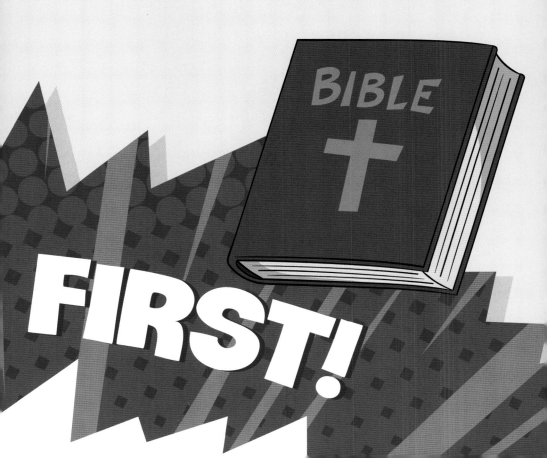

Kam smiled humbly as J2 and Kelsey rubbed his head, proud of their brother.

12

Skateland Fakers

It was a beautiful day as the Evans family arrived at the local skate park, one they had never visited before. Everyone was surprised to watch Tyson drop down a half-pipe with ease.

"When did Tyson learn to skateboard like that?" Kelsey asked.

Kam and Kylar ran off to get their helmets and skateboards, leaving J2 and Kelsey behind at the snack bar.

"Who wants to roll around on a dumb piece of wood?" Kelsey complained.

As Kam and Kylar looked over the edge of the steep ramp, they were suddenly bumped by another skater. They flew down the ramp and up the other side. Finally, they rolled backward, hit a bump, and crashed into a pile.

Everyone pointed and laughed at Kam and Kylar, including J2 and Kelsey.

Mr. Evans helped Kam and Kylar up off the ground and encouraged them to keep practicing.

J2 and Kelsey were surprised to see their best friends, Kirk and Paige.

"Paige! What are you guys doing here?" Kelsey asked.

"Grab your boards and come join us," invited Paige.

J2 and Kelsey looked nervous as they approached the edge of the ramp with their skateboards.

"We can do this," Kelsey muttered anxiously.

Kelsey and J2 closed their eyes and dropped down the ramp. When they opened their eyes, they realized they were headed for another ramp.

"How do you stop these things?!" J2 screamed.

J2 and Kelsey hit the ramp and were launched high into the air. They fell back down and slid to a stop at the bottom of the ramp.

The pair looked up to see everyone laughing at them, including Kirk and Paige. The only ones not laughing were the Evans family.

J2 and Kelsey sat on the bench, embarrassed. Mr. Evans approached and asked, "Are you guys hurt?"

"Just my pride," Kelsey responded.

"Well, I have to say, you had it coming," said Mr. Evans.

"How did we deserve to have everyone laughing at us?" demanded J2.

"Well, you guys have laughed at all the others who have fallen today," Mr. Evans explained.

"Oh, yeah," remembered Kelsey.

"It doesn't feel very good, does it?" Mr. Evans asked.

"Not at all," responded J2.

"Maybe there's something you guys can do to apologize," Mr. Evans suggested.

"Are you thinking what I'm thinking?" J2 asked Kelsey.

"Let's do it!" responded Kelsey.

J2 and Kelsey began to look for people who needed help.

A young boy fell off his skateboard. J2 and Kelsey ran and helped him back up.

Kelsey helped Bunny balance on her skateboard, while J2 assisted Kam. They helped a lot of skaters that day, and all were very thankful.

"It's a lot more fun encouraging people than laughing at them," Kelsey observed.

"Yeah, this is really fun!" responded J2.

By the end of the day, Bunny and Tyson were flying up and down the ramps together.

That night, all the kids were piled onto their parents' bed for storytime.

Mr. Evans shared, "Today I was reminded of a Scripture in Matthew 7 that says, 'Why worry about a speck in your friend's eye when you have a log in your own? How can you think of saying to your friend, "Let me help you get rid of that speck in your eye," when you can't see past the log in your own eye? Hypocrite! First get rid of the log in your own eye; then you will see well enough to deal with the speck in your friend's eye.'"

"How do you get a log in your eye?" Kam asked.

"Well, Kam, the Bible is talking about being blinded by your own pride. Pride is when you think you're better than other people. And when people think they're better than others, they tend to judge them," Mr. Evans explained.

"Like when I was laughing at Kam and Kylar for not know-ing how to ride down the ramps. I didn't know how to ride either. I was being a hypocrite," observed Kelsey.

"Let's remember that Jesus wants us to love people instead of judging them. He wants us to encourage others instead of laughing at them. We share Jesus's love when we do that. And it's the best feeling of all," Mr. Evans concluded.

"Hey, where's Bunny?" Mrs. Evans asked.

Bunny was at the top of the stairs with her skateboard. She pulled her helmet straps tight, hopped up on the handrail, and rode all the way down with beautiful form.

Conclusion

THANK YOU for allowing us the privilege of helping you teach your kids a few stories from the Storyteller. We pray that this book will help them fall in love with God's Word and apply it to their lives so they can influence their generation. Keep your eyes out for more Stories from the Storyteller™ resources!

Jonathan Evans is a mentor, author, speaker, and former NFL fullback. He treasures his relationship with Christ and uses his life to glorify God and to impact people by equipping and encouraging them in their faith.

A graduate of Dallas Theological Seminary with a master's degree in Christian Leadership, Jonathan serves with his pastor, friend, and father, Dr. Tony Evans, both in the local church and the national ministry of The Urban Alternative. They also teamed up together to write *Get in the Game*, a practical guidebook filled with sports analogies and spiritual truths aimed at strengthening readers with the skills they need for living victoriously. Jonathan serves as the chaplain of the Dallas Cowboys and co-chaplain of the Dallas Mavericks. He and his wife, Kanika, are the proud parents of Kelsey, Jonathan II, Kamden, Kylar, and Jade Wynter. They reside in Dallas, Texas.

Todd Hampson is a speaker, illustrator, animation producer, and the bestselling author of The Non-Prophet's Guide™ book series. His award-winning animation company, Timbuktoons, has produced content for many well-known ministry organizations. Todd and his wife are the proud parents of three grown children and make their home in Georgia.

watch These stories come to Life!

12:37 / 21:53

The **Stories from the Storyteller™** animated series is now available online. To learn more about this series and how your church can sign up to watch it, go to…

rightnow MEDIA **.COM**

TONYEVANS.ORG/STORIES